ME AND MY FRIENDSHIPS

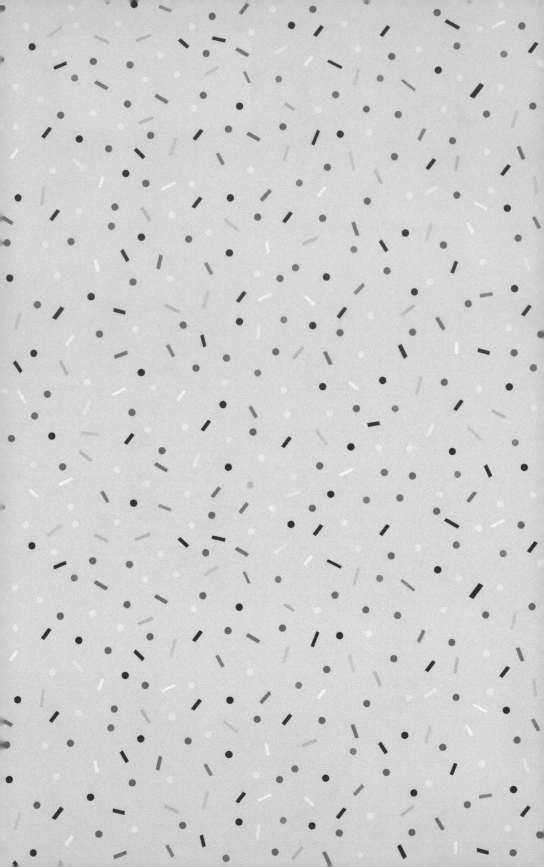

ME and MY MY FRIENDSHIPS

A Kid's Guide to Making and Being Friends

JOANN CROHN

Illustrations by Louie Chin

ROCKRIDGE
PRESS

Series Designer: Liz Cosgrove
Interior and Cover Designer: Karmen Lizzul
Art Producer: Sara Feinstein
Editor: Barbara J. Isenberg
Production Editor: Emily Sheehan
Production Manager: Jose Olivera

Illustrations © 2021 Louie Chin

ISBN: Print 978-1-64876-808-8 | eBook 978-1-64876-234-5
R0

CONTENTS

A LETTER TO GROWN-UPS

Welcome! I'm so happy you picked up this book. Right now, you may be wishing you could teach your child the social skills they need to be bolder, kinder, and happier in friendships. Maybe your heart sinks when your child tells you how lonely they are at school. Perhaps you feel your child is too bossy, but not sure how to encourage turn-taking and listening to others.

Maybe you're looking for some way to help your child brush up on the social skills they *do* have so that they feel more confident. Perhaps you wish your child knew what to avoid in friendships so they're not taken advantage of. Or you might want your child to be a kind person; one that includes others.

No matter what led you to pick up this book, I can tell you this: You, my friend, are in the right place. This book will not only teach your kids the social skills they need to make friendships, but it will also tell them how to keep those friendships strong.

First, we'll dive into what makes a good friend. Once kids define this for themselves, they're better able to work toward behaving in that way. Kids need a clear goal. By exploring friendship essentials as well as what kind of qualities they want in a friend, they create a vivid image of what kind of friend they want and want to be.

Then we'll explore their own personal reactions to friendship situations. Being able to stay calm and flexible as well as know how to self-regulate strong emotions not only improves relationships, but it also helps kids develop empathy. Research has shown that you can't tune into the emotions of others if you're consumed by your own reactions.

Next, we'll shift our focus to others. Kids will learn how to be active listeners in conversations as well as about the importance of kindness. Thinking of others and respecting differences is also key in developing empathy.

We'll also talk about group dynamics and how to be an includer.

Finally, we'll tackle those tricky situations such as gossiping, peer pressure, and bullying. Kids will feel more confident if they know that this happens and they have a strong game plan to deal with it.

A LETTER TO KIDS

Hi! Welcome to this book! I'm so happy you're here.

Right now, you may be wondering why kids play together at recess and leave you out.

Perhaps you feel nervous asking others to play. Or maybe talking to people feels very hard.

Nothing is wrong with you. You just haven't yet learned the skills for making and keeping friends. That's what you'll learn in this book.

It's important to have friends, because they help when you need it. They talk online with you when you're stuck at home. They play hide-and-seek with you on the playground.

Have you ever been the new kid? Or maybe you've started school and didn't know anyone?

After reading this book, you'll know how to introduce yourself to new people.

Have your friends ever said mean things to you? Have they left you out? That's not your fault. I'm going to show you what to look for in a friend.

Sometimes big emotions get in the way of friend-ships. You'll learn how to calm down when you get mad. When you're calm, you can see what your friend needs from you.

Then you'll learn how to talk with friends. This is a big one! I used to think that friends would like me more if I told them all kinds of interesting stuff. Not true! Friends feel happier when you show interest in *them*. That shows them you care, and that's important for a good friendship.

You'll finish this book knowing exactly how to make and keep better friends. You'll feel more confident talking to others and asking people to play. Let's get started!

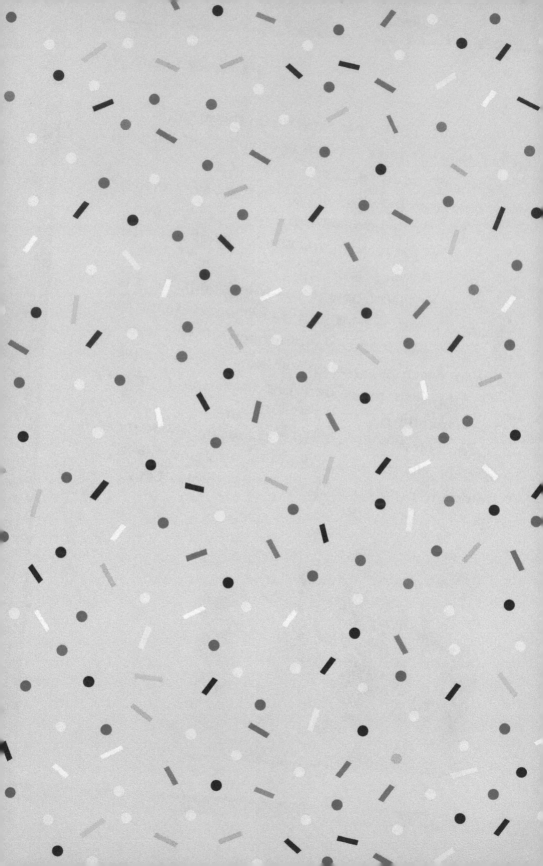

1.
THE ROAD
TO
FRIENDSHIP

Why do some kids have an easy time making friends? They always have someone to talk to. They're playing games with other kids on the playground. It seems so simple for them! Do you ever wish you were more like that?

It's okay. The truth is, making friends isn't easy for everyone. It's not magic that you're born with. I'm going to tell you a secret: A lot of adults have a hard time making friends, too!

But I have good news! Making friends is a skill. It's like riding a bike, baking chocolate chip cookies, or beating a level on a video game. Do you know how to ride a bike the first time you jump on? No way! First, you learn the steps. Then you practice, practice, practice. That's it. I know you can do this! Just like riding a bike, you may not be good at these skills right away. That's okay. I expect that. I don't want you to give up when it's hard. You will get better and better the more you practice. Your brain will start growing with new friendship know-how.

In this chapter, we start our journey. Let's teach our brains how to use new friendship skills.

WHAT MAKES A GOOD FRIEND?

Good friends are all around you. You see them every day. You just don't know them well . . . yet.

Friends can sometimes be hard to spot. Are they the group of kids who play soccer every day? Is it that girl who quietly sits by herself and reads? What about the kids talking to one another in the corner?

What makes a good friend? A good friend is kind to you. They help you out when you're feeling sad. Good friends don't make you feel bad on purpose. They're also honest. A good friend doesn't lie to you or laugh at you when you're not around. They are fair and trustworthy.

You want to find a friend who listens to you when you have a problem. A good friend will try to help you out every way they can. Friends support each other during the happy times. They care about each other during tough times. Good friends listen. Good friends cheer you on. Good friends don't want to see you hurt.

First, you need to know what you want in a friend. Then you need to take the first step.

If you're thinking, oh my gosh, I'm too shy to do that! Don't worry. We're going to work on it.

What Kind of Friends Do I Want?

Before you start making friends, let's stop and think about what you want. You want a friend who is kind to you. You want a friend who sees you on the playground and waves. You want a friend who says nice things to you. Also, you want a friend who is nice to other people.

Think a little more about what makes a good friend. Circle the answers that best describe what you want in a friend.

1. You just tripped over a backpack in the middle of class. You want a friend who:

   a. Asks if you're okay.

   b. Makes a joke about how klutzy you are and laughs.

2. You're playing soccer on the playground. You want a friend who:

   a. Gives you a turn to kick the ball.

   b. Keeps the ball to themself and passes to only one other person.

3. You see your friend talking with a group of friends. Your friend:

    a. Invites you over to join them.

    b. Ignores you and keeps talking.

4. You ask your friend what they did this weekend. They:

    a. Tell you what they did and then ask you about your weekend.

    b. Keep talking on and on. They never even ask about you!

Mostly A's: You want a friend who is kind and thinks of you. They're honest and trustworthy. This is a great friend to have!

Mostly B's: Even though your friend might seem popular, they're not acting kind. It's hard to be happy with a friend like that. But it's okay. This book will help you know what to look for in a friend.

A mix of A's and B's: That's normal! This book will celebrate what's going right and you'll learn what you might want to change.

What Would You Do?

Being a good friend takes work. We all make mistakes. Read these short friendship stories. Decide if the person is being a good friend. Then explain what you would do.

Alex is friends with Carmen. He always hears Carmen saying mean things about other people. Carmen made fun of a classmate's drawing. She laughed at another kid at recess. She won't let Alex's friend Daniel sit at the lunch table.

Is Carmen being a good friend? What would you do if you were Alex?

_____

Javier wrote a story. He worked hard and he's super excited. It has all of his favorite things: aliens, rocket ships, and magic. He asks his friend Allen to read it. Allen reads the first few pages. "This is amazing! You worked so hard on this!" he says.

Is Allen being a good friend? What would you say to Javier?

_____

Cam is eating lunch in the school cafeteria. It's pizza day. She sits down by her friend Sondra. She sees two other friends, Sky and Isabel, sitting at the end of the table. She waves hi to them. Sky and Isabel whisper something to each other. Then they laugh and turn around. Cam feels ignored.

Are Sky and Isabel being good friends?

Audrey and Daniella are in art class together. They're sharing Audrey's markers to draw. The teacher announces that it's time to pack up to go home. The markers are all over the table. Some are even on the floor. Daniella stops drawing and helps Audrey pick up all the markers.

Is Daniella being a good friend? What would you do if you were Daniella?

FRIENDSHIP BASICS

Now you know what you want in a friend, so it's time to start working on *being* a good friend. These are the friendship basics! They're also called social skills.

Social skills are what we use to communicate with other people. They are **what** you say and **how** you say it.

To be a great friend, you need to:

Listen well: You can better remember what people say when you listen well. If your friend says, "I really like hamburgers, but I think hot dogs are gross," you shouldn't be sitting there dreaming about pizza! Instead, you should be thinking, "Oh, my friend

doesn't like hot dogs." You get better at listening by trying to repeat back what your friend says.

Include others: Think about a group playing soccer on the playground. You want to play, but no one invites you. That stinks, right? We want to include others. The next time you're with other kids, look around you. Is someone sitting alone? Invite them to sit with you.

Take turns: Have you ever been friends with someone who doesn't share? It feels lousy. Friends take turns talking and playing. Each friend has fun instead of only one person.

Smile: This is a big one! Friends make each other feel good. The easiest way to make someone feel good is to smile. A smile is like a huge welcome sign. It shows others that you want to talk to them.

Be trustworthy: Has a kid ever said he liked your backpack, then five seconds later you hear him tell someone else, "That backpack is ugly!"? He's just showed you he's not trustworthy. Being trustworthy means you can trust what your friend says and does.

Be kind: Being kind means doing good for others. You're kind when you offer to play an online game with your friend. Writing to your friend when they don't feel well is kind, too. These little actions make friendships feel good.

What Kind of Friend Do I Want to Be?

Let's think about some of the qualities you have—or want to work on—to be a good friend. Circle all the words you think describe you NOW.

Trustworthy

Good listener

Kind

Friendly

Includes others

Takes turns

Generous

Fun

Good problem-solver

Playful

Adventurous

Helpful

Respectful

Cooperative

Happy for your friends

Choose one of the words you circled. Fill in the blanks in this sentence.

I am _____

when I _____.

Now circle the qualities you want to work on.

Trustworthy

Good Listener

Kind

Friendly

Includes others

Takes turns

Generous

Fun

Good problem-solver

Playful

Adventurous

Helpful

Respectful

Cooperative

Happy for your friends

Choose one of the words you circled. Fill in the following blanks. Explain what you can do to work on that skill.

I can be more _____

by _____.

ALL ABOUT ME

We have one more step before we start making friends. I want you to think about who YOU are and what YOU like to do. You want friends who like some of the same things you like (at least at first). When you know what you like and do those things, it's easier to find friends who like the same things. Let's figure out more about you!

Do you like to be quiet or loud?

Maybe it's a little bit of both. Is your favorite activity curling up on a sunny chair reading a book? Or do you like to laugh and shout in a game of tag?

What interests you?

You have nothing to do on a Saturday afternoon. Let's make some plans! What will you choose?

Maybe it's playing video games, or having friends come to your house. Maybe you want to do something active, like riding your bike around your neighborhood or throwing a Frisbee in the park.

Are you creative?

Is a big painting project exciting to you? Or maybe it's making something with your hands, like building a rocket or decorating your room?

When I was a kid, I loved to act and be on stage. Many of my friends loved that, too, and we would write plays and make up our own skits.

Do you like being outdoors or indoors?

Is a hike through the woods, and then sitting by a fire and roasting marshmallows, your favorite thing in the world? Instead, maybe you like being busy inside, playing board games or hide-and-seek, or building something.

Do you have a special talent?

Do you play the piano, drums, or another musical instrument? Can you rap? Do you take songs you hear and make up your own words to the melody? Are you the best joke-teller in your family? What do you like to do that other people tell you is amazing?

Did you learn a new skill lately that you're super excited about? Think about that! Did you beat a new level in a game? Or do a cartwheel?

I hope these questions helped you think more about what you like to do.

What Do I Like to Do?

Now that you're thinking about what you like, let's write things down! Answer the following questions.

Circle the words that describe you:

Funny	Calm
Honest	Caring
Helpful	Quiet
Kind	Strong
Organized	Fair

Would you rather . . . (circle one from each row)

- Hike in the woods *or* play in a park?
- Play video games *or* play hide-and-seek?
- Build a fort *or* do crafts?
- Go to a big party *or* spend time with a friend one-on-one?
- Read a book *or* watch a movie?
- Act in a play *or* write a play?
- Eat something sweet *or* eat something sour?
- Sit with a group at school *or* sit alone?
- Know everything in the world *or* be able to make anyone laugh?

Answer the following questions:

What do you love doing that makes you happy?

_____

What can you teach others?

_____

What are you grateful for?

_____

What's the best thing that's ever happened to you?

_____

What's the worst thing that's happened to you?

_____

If you could change the world,
what would you do?

_____

_____

_____

REMEMBER THIS

The only way to get good at making friends is to practice. Try these ideas to practice your new skills. Ask your parent or another grown-up to pretend to be another kid.

I want you to practice:

- Inviting someone to join you at lunch
- Taking turns in a game
- Introducing yourself to someone you don't know
- Solving the problem (on your own) of what to do when a friend doesn't share the ball at recess and it makes you mad

YOU DID IT!

You finished the first chapter! Time for a dance party! I hope you're doing your favorite dance moves right now. You need to celebrate.

I want to remind you of what you just did. You learned:

- Good friends support and listen to you. They are kind and make you feel good.
- What you want to look for in a friend
- Friendship skills, including:

  › taking turns

  › listening

  › smiling

  › including others

  › being kind

- The kind of friend that you want to be
- What you like to do, so you can find friends who like the same things

In the next chapter, I'll teach you how to be the best YOU. Our friends love us when we're kind. But being kind all the time isn't always simple. It's easy to get mad. It's hard to control your emotions. You can't be your best self when you're angry. That's why I'll show you how to calm down when you get upset.

2.
BEING THE BEST YOU

Nobody expects you to be perfect, especially not your friends, but there are a few things you can do to make sure things go well. You'll make mistakes sometimes, and that's okay! I'm going to show you how to put your best self forward in this chapter. For example, have you ever felt so mad that you wanted to yell? Maybe you were playing a game on the playground and someone cheated. That would make me pretty mad! Or maybe you stomped off the playground because you didn't get a turn on the swings? Yup. I get that.

Maybe you hide your feelings about what you like. You let other people have a turn and you never get to do what you want to do. This means that friends never get the chance to know the real you. That hurts, right? It makes you feel left out when you agree to someone else's games and they never want to play your games.

Those are all big emotions! We're going to talk about ways to handle these situations. It's totally okay to make mistakes. Everyone does! I'll show you how to get through them and be your best you.

EXPRESSING YOURSELF

The best way to make great friends is to know yourself and how to express yourself. Expressing yourself means sharing what you like and don't like with other people. When you know what you like to do and are able to share that with others, you can find friends who like the same things. Remember the "All About Me" activity we did in the last chapter (page 12)? That should have given you some clues about what you like to do. If so, you are ready to share that with other people. Here's how.

Look for people who like the same activities you do. If you like being super active, look for friends on the playground who are running and climbing. If you like quiet games, look for the kids who are talking off to the side.

Share what you like! Don't hide it. When we hide who we are, we're unhappy. It feels as if we always have to do stuff for other people and that no one cares about us. It can feel pretty rotten and lonely. That's why it's important to share what you like.

For instance, you can say:

"You're reading *Dogman*! I like *Dogman*, too."

"You chose pizza for lunch. I like pizza, too."

"Your game looks fun! I like playing basketball, too."

Practice finding that one little thing you have in common with someone else and then share what you like about it, too.

Ask questions. When you ask questions, you're trying to find out what new friends like so that you can find something in common. You also share a little bit about yourself.

For example:

> **"I went to a fun restaurant this weekend. Did you do anything fun?"**
>
> **"I played *Tycoon* on Roblox. Do you play on Roblox?"**
>
> **"I watched a really funny movie last night. What's your favorite funny movie?"**

Asking questions can at first seem really scary. Try a few that are easy for you and then go from there. It will get easier with practice.

What Would You Do?

Here are some friendship situations in which kids express themselves to others. Some will be good examples of how to express yourself and others will be examples of how not to express yourself.

In the following situations, decide who is expressing themselves well and what you would do.

Janie sees a group of girls chatting in the corner of the playground. They're talking all about their favorite dolls. "I like Malibu Cindy with the pink hair," one says. Janie doesn't know what dolls they're talking about. She nods her head and doesn't say anything. When another girl asks which doll she likes, Janie says, "Oh, I like all of them."

Is Janie showing how to or how not to express yourself? _____

What would you do? _____

_____

Jeremiah is talking with a group in class. He talks nonstop and tells the group everything he did last summer. "I went to a water park and went on the biggest slide! Then we went camping in the woods. I learned how to build a fire and put up a tent." The other kids in his group don't look interested. But Jeremiah keeps talking. He doesn't ask them any questions about themselves or let anyone else talk.

Is Jeremiah showing how to or how not to express yourself? _____

What would you do? _____

Erik is eating lunch with his friends in the cafeteria. A new boy in class, James, comes up to them. "Hey, can I eat with you?" he asks. "Sure," Erik says. "Oooh, mac and cheese! I love that!" James says. Erik replies, "Yeah, it's my favorite."

Is James showing how to or how not to express yourself? _____

What would you do? _____

_____

CALM AND COOL

Have you ever gotten so angry that you've yelled at someone? I know that I have!

It's possible you don't yell when you're angry. Maybe you shut down and stomp away. I can get like that, too. In each situation, our emotions are in control instead of our thinking brains. Controlling emotions is like floating down a river. Imagine you're in a tube or a raft floating calmly. Up ahead, you see some rocks in the river, so you paddle to one side. But be careful. Don't hit the shore!

That's what your emotions are like. Every time something makes you upset, those are the rocks.

You try to steer around them, but you have to be careful not to lose control and get angry. That's like hitting the shore. It's important to stay calm and control your strong emotions. Believe it or not, that makes it easier to make and keep friends.

Friends don't like being yelled at. They don't like being blamed. And they don't like others saying mean things to them. These things can all happen when you're angry. I know you don't want to ruin a friendship because of things you said and did when you were upset. So you need to control your strong emotions. Here's how.

Find a grown-up you trust to talk with

Do you know an adult you can talk with about your feelings? Maybe it's your parents. Or it could be an aunt, uncle, grandparent, or even an older sibling. Find this person when you get upset, and tell them why you're angry. This isn't you telling on your friend. Instead, you're asking the adult for help calming down.

Stop and take a break

Know when you're about to "hit the shore." If you feel your emotions getting out of control, you can stop and take a break. If you think a friend is cheating in a game, stop and walk away. This will give you time to think and cool down. If you get frustrated when trying to write something, put down your pencil and take a deep breath.

Take a Belly Breath

When adults tell you to take a deep breath, where does the air go? Have you ever thought about that? I can say that most people breathe all the air into their chest. That does nothing to calm them down! In fact, it probably makes them feel more upset. Instead, you're going to learn how to breathe into your belly. You will need a small toy for this. A stuffed animal will work perfectly.

Here's what to do:

1. Lie on your back on the floor. Pick a room where you feel good and can relax.

2. Place the stuffed animal on your belly.

3. Breathe in through your nose.

4. Watch the stuffed animal rise up toward the sky.

5. Very slowly, breathe out through your mouth. Be sure to breathe slowly so your stuffed animal goes down slowly.

When you breathe out, it's important to remember your stuffed animal does not like going down fast. It scares them. You don't want to scare them. So, when you breathe out, do it slowly—so slowly that your stuffed animal isn't scared.

Now breathe in through your nose again. Make it long and slow. Remember how scared your animal friend gets! Breathe out slowly again. Keep doing this. Do you feel how your body relaxes? You may even feel a bit sleepy after a few minutes.

That's a belly breath!

FLEXIBLE THINKING

Don't you wish you could always get what you want? The world would be so easy! Can you imagine?

You say, "I want to play hide-and-seek" and everyone agrees.

You say, "I want to color right now" and all your friends do it with you.

Nope. It doesn't work that way. Our friends also want turns to do what they want. We need to do what our friends want to make sure they feel happy in the friendship, too. In good friendships, both people get a little of what they want. They also give up a little of what they want to make the other person happy. And we want to make others happy, right? So we do something called flexible thinking. Think about a superhero. She bends. She twists. She gets out of the way of danger fast. She's flexible—which means she's able to change her plans when she needs to.

Think about the last time you and your friends couldn't decide what to do. Now imagine your friend wants to play golf with a basketball and you want to play a game on your tablet. What do you do? You need to be flexible. One way to do this is to try a "Give and Take."

First, "Give": You can say to your friend, "Okay, we can try playing golf with a basketball." You're giving your friend what they want.

Then you ask for your "Take": "After we do that, can we play a game on the tablet?" You're also asking for what you want.

Your friend may say yes or they may have another idea that you like just as much. The important thing is that you offered to do something that wasn't your first choice.

Pretend you really want to watch a movie but your friend wants to play hide-and-seek. You need to use your flexible thinking here.

You can say to your friend: "I don't feel like running around right now. Is there something else you want to do instead?"

The most important thing is that you're telling your friend what you don't want to do. This is so important! We wish people could have superpower mind-reading skills, but they don't. You're also thinking about your friend, by trying to do something they want to do.

What's a Good Solution?

It may be hard to figure out a solution that makes both you and your friend happy. You might do things that always make your friend happy and never ask for what you want. This isn't good. Remember, in friendships it's important that both people feel happy. You may have trouble thinking in a flexible way and never let your friend get what they want. That's not good, either.

So we're going to practice.

In the following quiz, circle the answer that is the best example of flexible thinking.

1. You invite your friend Juliette over to play. You are so excited about your new slime craft kit, but Juliette doesn't like slime. Instead, she wants to watch a movie. What do you do?

   a. Ask Juliette if there is another craft she wants to do instead. You can also use your chalk hair color.

   b. Tell her you only want to do slime . . . nothing else. It's your house. Your rules.

   c. Decide that since Juliette is a guest, you should do what she wants to do. You're not excited about watching a movie, but you do it anyway.

2. You're playing with a new friend on the playground. They love the swings, but you've been swinging all

morning and you're bored. You would like to race them on the slides. What do you do?

a. Ask your friend if they can swing on the swings for a little bit and then do a race on the slides.

b. Tell your friend that you're done on the swings. Nope. No more. You're leaving.

c. Keep swinging even though you're bored.

3. You just got a new skateboard. Your friend Brooklyn doesn't like skateboarding. She wants to throw a softball around. What do you do?

a. Ask Brooklyn, "Is there anything else you would like to do?" Softball isn't your thing.

b. Stomp off mad. You never get to do what you want!

c. Say you'll play softball. At least Brooklyn came to play with you.

Mostly A's: You are using great flexible thinking. Keep it up!

Mostly B's: You should also be thinking about what your friend wants to do. Use that to come up with a solution that works for you.

Mostly C's: You're trying to be nice to your friend. But you're ignoring what you like. It's okay to ask to do something else!

WHEN TO BE A COMEDIAN

Have you ever tried to be funny but it made your friends mad? Has something like this ever happened? Maybe your friend was walking to get something in class and they tripped. Your friend always trips over something! When they fell, they made a funny noise and laughed about it. Later at lunch, you say something like: "Oh my gosh, when you fell, it looked like a monkey flying through the air. Like those flying monkeys! Ahahahahah!!" The corners of your friend's mouth turn down and they look away. They don't talk to you or look you in the eye. Your friend is hurt.

But you thought it was funny! You thought they thought it was funny when they tripped, because they laughed about it when it happened. Now they're mad at you.

"I was just kidding," you say. Nope. That didn't help. What do you do?

Sometimes it's okay to be a comedian, and other times it's not. It's hard to figure out the correct time. You'll make mistakes with this, and that's okay. What do you do when this happens?

Step 1: Notice your friend's face
When people are upset, a few things happen. You might have seen this in the story. The corners of

a person's mouth turn down. It might not be a big frown. Sometimes it's a little change. It could be they were smiling before, and now their mouth is a thin, straight line. They may also look down or look away. These are all signs they're mad. Once you notice they're mad, you can move to the second step.

Step 2: Apologize

Really apologize. Saying, "I'm just kidding" is not apologizing. In fact, saying, "I'm just kidding" takes away someone's right to be upset. It's like saying, "You shouldn't be upset; it was just a joke." But they *are* upset and, as a friend, you should apologize.

Say something like: "I'm sorry I hurt your feelings." That's all you need to say.

The next time you think you're being funny, but you realize you hurt your friend's feelings, it's okay. You will make mistakes. You will make jokes that other people feel hurt by. Say, "I'm sorry" and try to fix what happened.

REMEMBER THIS

The next time you feel you're being funny but no one laughs, remember these simple steps.

- Watch your friend's face. Do the corners of their mouth turn down? Do they go from smiling to their mouth stretched into one straight line? Do they look down? If so, they're upset.

- Apologize. "I'm sorry I hurt your feelings" is all you need to say.

- Think about what you want other people to do when they hurt you. Would you like them to say "I'm sorry"? Can you say or do anything else to fix it? Does your friend like hugs? Can you offer to do something for her?

YOU DID IT!

You made it to the end of another chapter! You are rocking this.

This chapter was all about how to be the best version of you. Now you know how to:

- Express yourself and not hide your true feelings about what you like to do. You'll find good friends when you're honest about what you like and don't like.

- Float down the stream of calm emotions and start to notice when you're about to hit the shore. If you're about to hit the shore, it's okay. Because now you know how to . . . take a belly breath.

- Do the belly breath! You practiced this! Lie down on the floor with a toy on your belly and let it take the ride down slowly.

You also learned how to use flexible thinking. Finding a solution where both you and your friend can be happy is important.

And you know now that if you make a joke that hurts someone's feelings, you can notice if they're upset and apologize.

You are learning more and more about what it takes to make and keep friends. Remember that these are skills. You're not going to be good at them all right away. But you're strong. I know you're going to keep going and keep practicing even though it may be hard.

3.

TALKING AND LISTENING

Psst. I have a secret.

I used to be scared to talk to other people.

No, really! I couldn't look them in the eye. I didn't know what to say. Every time I had to go someplace new, my stomach got all tied up in knots.

When I grew up, I learned that a lot of people have this problem. If you don't know what to say to new friends, you're normal!

My problem didn't go away as a grown-up, either. I still get nervous meeting new people. But I have some tricks now. There is one big secret about knowing what to say to others. Ready?

People want to feel listened to. That's it. You don't have to impress them. You don't need to know what to say all the time. You just have to listen.

In this chapter, you'll learn:

What to say

What to do with your body

How to show other people you're listening to them

We're going to make you feel good about talking and listening to other people. Let's get started!

GETTING GOOD AT TALKING

Let's face it: Sometimes talking with others is hard. It's tough to know just what to say. Do you ever get mad when someone talks over you? You have this great story you're telling about your weekend. Then your classmate starts telling a story about their dog. Or, even worse, they ask the person you're talking with to swing on the swings. Rude.

Remember how I said most people want to feel listened to? Being a good listener makes you a better talker. The next time you talk with someone else, look out for these things.

Take turns talking and listening

Have you talked to someone and they kept talking and talking and talking? They didn't want to hear about you. They never asked you a single question. Were you bored? Probably.

That's why we need to take turns talking and listening. We don't want other people to feel bored talking with us. How do we do this?

Ask people questions about themselves

Questions make every conversation better! These can be very simple, such as:

• What did you do this weekend?

- What book are you reading?
- What do you have for lunch?

Stay on topic

Have you ever been talking about something really interesting to you and someone changes the subject? Frustrating, right? That's why we need to finish talking about one thing before changing subjects.

By taking turns talking and listening, asking questions, and staying on topic, you can make sure everyone feels listened to.

REMEMBER THIS

See someone new whom you want to talk with? Keep these three things in mind.

1. Start by saying something you like about them. This is a trick I use all the time! You can say something simple, like "I like your shoes." Or, you can say something nice about what they did, like "I liked your drawing in class."

2. Then ask a question. If you gave them a compliment about their shoes, you can ask, "Where did you get them?" If you said something nice about their drawing, you can ask, "Do you draw a lot?"

3. See where it goes from there!

Conversation Dos and Don'ts

Phew! All these new conversation tips can get confusing! Wouldn't it be handy to have a list of Dos and Don'ts? Yes? Well, here you go!

Do:

- **Ask questions.** Questions are always good, because they let you learn more about other people.
- **Watch how people react.** Look at their face when you're talking. That's how you can tell if they're really happy to talk about something or if they're bored.
- **Try to find something you have in common.** That's how to really keep a conversation going. Find something you like just as much as the other person. Then you can talk and talk and talk with them.
- **Compliment them.** People want to feel liked. They want to feel listened to. Find something you like about another person and tell them. It's gold. Watch as they smile.

Don't:

- **Make it all about you.** Everyone wants a chance to share. Ask someone a question about themself if you find you're talking too much about yourself.
- **Change the topic suddenly.** Imagine you're talking about your favorite movie. You're telling how the fireworks burst over the invisible jet. All of a sudden, your friend starts talking about a video game. WHAT?!? You feel ignored. That's not how you want to make someone else feel.
- **Keep talking and talking.** Remember the feeling you have when someone else keeps talking and doesn't ask you any questions? You want to say something, but you can't! Give other people a chance to speak.
- **Complain.** Complaining is not conversation. When you say, "Class is so boring" or "No one ever lets me have a turn," it's no fun for anyone. Instead, try to focus on the positive.

BE AN ACTIVE LISTENER

Most people don't listen. It's true. It's a bad habit so many people have—even adults! They look as if they're listening, but really they're just thinking of what to say next. Do you ever do this? I do. That's why I used to be so nervous in conversations. I worried so much about saying the right thing that I didn't listen very well.

How can you be a good active listener?

1. **Look people in the eye.**
   It's hard to think of other things when you're watching someone's face. If you get too shy while looking someone in the eyes, that's okay. You can look at the space right between their eyes. They'll think you're looking in their eyes. Having some place to look will help you listen better.

2. **Repeat what they say before you talk.**

   I do this all the time. It helps me make sure I heard the other person right. It also gives me time to think of what to say.

   Here's how it works. Pretend you're talking to your friend about jelly beans. Your friend is telling you how they like the cream soda flavor, but not the buttered popcorn flavor. And ew! Those flavor beans, who wants to eat grass or vomit? You can say, "So you like the sweet flavors but you don't like the weird flavors." You repeated what they said in your own words. They know you listened to them. You can then say something like, "I kind of like buttered popcorn. But yeah, those weird flavors are gross."

3. **Hold back your monster judge.**

   Have you ever talked with someone and they said, "That's silly. Why would you do that?" That person did not hold back their monster judge. It's that inside voice that wants to tell other people how wrong they are. While it's okay to disagree, there's a kind way to do it. The monster judge doesn't care about kindness. All it cares about is being right.

   If you feel your monster judge wants to say something about what someone likes or dislikes, hold back! Let your friend speak and then disagree kindly, the way we did about the jelly beans.

Yes or No

Let's test your active listening skills! Here are some examples of people talking.

You can circle YES if the example shows active listening or NO if it doesn't.

Jeremy is talking to his friend Tasha. While Tasha talks, Jeremy looks at the space right between Tasha's eyes.

YES   NO

Evie is working on a project with two of her classmates. They're supposed to make a poster about volcanoes. Evie starts telling her classmates about the bug she found on the playground.

YES   NO

Carlos is telling his friend Alek about his weekend. While Carlos talks, Alek watches the soccer game on the playground.

YES   NO

Jenni tells her friend Yvette about a drawing she's working on. She describes the colors and the paints and what brushes she's using. Yvette then says to Jenni, "Wow, you're using a lot of colors and cool brushes. You sound really excited."

YES   NO

OUR BODIES TALK, TOO

It's not just what we say to people, it's what our bodies do, too. You may not realize it, but our bodies talk just as much as our mouths.

Here are some ways that your body talks.

Eye contact

We've talked about this before. When you look some-one in the eyes, they know you're paying attention to them. You are focused on them. Remember that if you feel a little shy, you can always look at the space between their eyes.

Tone of voice

The tone of our voice has a lot to do with our bodies. Your voice is made by your vocal cords. These are muscles in your throat that make your voice sound low or high or shaky or strong.

When you are nervous, your vocal cords get tight. That makes your voice sound high. When you relax, your vocal cords loosen up, making your voice lower.

This low and high is the tone of your voice. You can tell someone's feelings by the tone of their voice. Your body is talking.

Body language

Your body can express how you feel. Sometimes, when a person has slumped shoulders, it means that they are sad.

Your body language can also show confidence. Stand up very tall and put your hands on your hips. How do you feel when you stand this way? Strong? You should! The way you stand makes you feel a certain way. It sends a message to other people.

Your face

You can tell a lot by looking at some-one's face. Are they smiling? Are they frowning? Is their mouth in a straight line? (This usually means they feel upset.)

Personal space

Sometimes people need space between them-selves and another person. Some people need more space than others. If you're talking to someone and they take a step back, it means they need more space between you and them. Don't step forward. Give them their space.

What Would You Do?

Let's practice being detectives. Instead of solving a mystery, I want you to figure out how someone else feels based on their body language.

Read each situation and answer the questions.

Camdyn is talking to her friend Faith about baking cookies. Faith loves baking! She's super excited. When Camdyn tells Faith they're making chocolate chip cookies, Faith's shoulders fall and she looks away. "Oh," she says, "okay."

How does Faith feel about making chocolate chip cookies? _____

Jessica and Jacqueline are working together on a class project. As Jacqueline talks about the Titanic, Jessica nods and smiles. Then Jacqueline talks about writing the paragraph for their project. She asks Jessica if she can type. Jessica looks down at her hands and then at the computer. She bites her lip. "I mean," she says, "I guess I can type."

How does Jessica feel about typing? _____
_____

YOU DID IT!

Time for another celebration! Did you learn a lot of new stuff about talking and listening? I hope so! Let's review.

You learned that talking is hard for lots of people. But it's good to remember to:

- Stay on topic. Don't start talking about what's for lunch in the middle of a friend telling you about their weekend.

- Ask questions. It shows you're interested in the other person. People love answering questions.

- Do not hog the conversation. If you feel yourself talking too much, look around. What do your friends' faces and body language look like? Can you ask someone a question?

We also talked about being an active listener. When you're an active listener, you:

- Make eye contact.

- Repeat what someone says in your own words.

Are you ready to try your new skills with a friend? Which one will you try first?

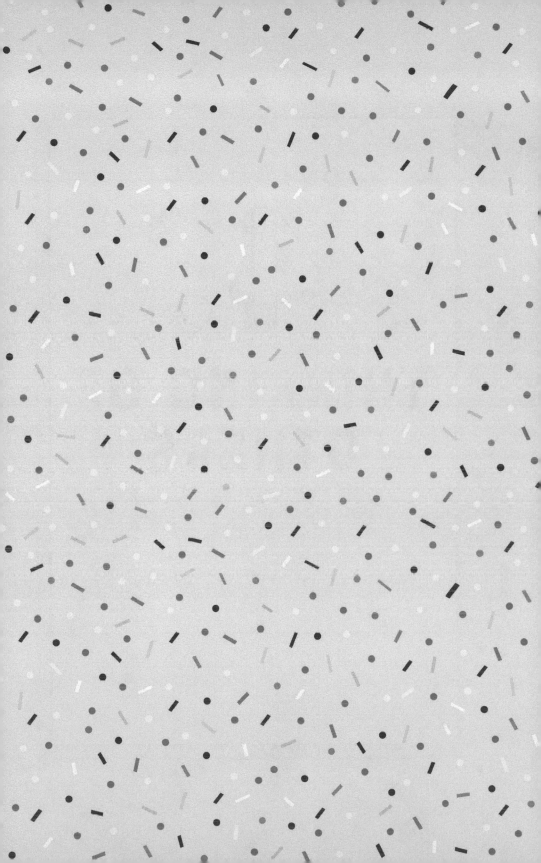

THINKING OF OTHERS

For us to be truly good friends, we need to think of others and their feelings. It helps us be kind and say the right things.

Have you heard about your kindness muscle? No? It takes a lot of work to grow the kindness muscle. You know how people lift weights to make muscles in their arms and legs grow big and strong? The same goes for your kindness muscle. You need to use it every day to get better at being kind. If you're not doing this now, it's okay. In this chapter you will learn about kind things you can do to help you think more about others. The best thing about kindness is that it makes you happier as well.

There are two things you need to do each day to exercise your kindness muscle. First, know that all acts of kindness are great! You can be kind face-to-face or on a video call, or you can leave a kind note for someone where they can find it.

Second, be kind without expecting anything. When you're kind, you don't do it because you expect others to be kind back. You do it because you're a kind person.

KINDNESS GOES A LONG WAY

What does it mean to be kind? You're kind when you're friendly, giving, and considerate. Considerate means that you care about other people and their feelings.

Remember in the last chapter when we talked about how people like to be listened to? That's a big part of being kind. It's listening to how other people feel and then doing something to help them.

One simple way to be kind is to smile at others.
Think about how you feel when you go to the grocery store with your grown-ups. Maybe you don't like grocery shopping, because it takes a long time. You don't want to go. But then you see someone from your school there. You don't know them well. They see you, too. They smile and wave. You wave back. It makes you feel pretty good, right? This simple way to be kind goes a long way.

Another way to be kind is helping someone when they're upset.
Pretend your friend feels sad about getting a bad grade on a math test. You can be kind to them by listening. You listen as your friend says they don't get it. They're trying to understand, but they don't know what to do. To be kind, you might offer to help them with math. Or you might ask, "What can I do for you?"

You can also be kind by listening to what other people want to do.
Maybe you're on the playground. Your friend wants to swing on the swings. But you would like to practice cartwheels. To be kind, you offer to swing for a little bit and ask if she'll do cartwheels with you afterward.

Kindness is finding something that everyone is happy with.

Kindness Checklist

Look at this list of kindness activities that you can do every day. Every little thing you do exercises your kindness muscle. Put a check next to the ones you want to try.

☐ Find someone new to smile at and say, "Good morning"

☐ Hold the door open for someone

☐ Tell someone a funny joke

☐ Call a family member who you haven't seen in a while

☐ Tell your friend something you like about them

☐ Let someone go ahead of you in line

☐ Set the table for dinner

☐ Pass out stickers to people

☐ Read a book to someone

☐ Help a friend pick up something they dropped

☐ Wave at kids you see in the park

☐ Share a toy with a friend

☐ Teach someone something new

☐ Congratulate someone and give them a high five

☐ Ask someone who looks lonely to eat or play with you

☐ Give your grown-up a hug

Write down which kind thing you'll try today:

Today, I will _____

WALK IN SOMEONE ELSE'S SNEAKERS

It can be hard to figure out how someone else feels. That's why we're going to practice walking in someone else's sneakers. This doesn't mean we're taking your friend's shoes and putting them on! Instead, we're going to think about another person's thoughts and feelings. We're practicing empathy. Empathy is when we try to understand what someone else is feeling.

Why do we need to do this? Paying attention to other people makes us better friends. Using empathy

helps us know if we should comfort our friends or try to make them laugh.

Here's how we can use empathy:

1. **Look at your friend's face.**

   A person's face gives you so many clues about how they feel.

   When you look at someone's face, pay attention to how you feel. Your brain does work behind the scenes, and you will feel a little of that person's emotions when you see the look on their face. When they frown, you'll feel a little sad, too. Pay attention to those feelings.

   If you say something and notice your friend's face looks hurt, you're allowed a do-over. Remember that it's okay to make mistakes. When you feel as if you've hurt someone, try something to make it better.

2. **Think about how you would feel.**

   Pretend your friend has lost their library book. They're digging through their backpack. Their eyebrows are crinkled up. Their mouth is in a frown.

   How would you feel if you lost something? Would you be nervous about getting in trouble? Would you be scared that people would be mad at you?

   Use those feelings to take the final step.

3. What can you do to help?

The best way to figure this out is to think what would make you feel better if this happened to you. Would you like help finding your library book? Would you like someone to tell you that it'll be okay?

Try that first. And it's okay if you make a mistake. The way we learn what other people like and feel is by trying. We'll never do it perfectly. Maybe your friend would rather find the library book by themself. That's okay. You are allowed a do-over. You can say, "I'm sorry. Can I do anything to help you?"

REMEMBER THIS

Look at people's faces to try to figure out what they might be feeling.

Imagine how you might feel in the same situation. This will help you decide what to do next.

Think to yourself, "I wonder what my friend needs right now."

What Would You Do?

It's time to practice your new skill of empathy. Read these stories and then decide what you think that person is feeling.

Henry is a new kid at school. He walks into class and you turn to look at him. He has plastic cuffs that run up the front of his legs and he uses crutches to walk. Your teacher introduces him to the class and says how much he loves mystery books and playing board games. You like those things, too! Henry is looking down at the floor. He's not making eye contact with anyone when the teacher introduces him.

How do you think Henry feels right now?

_____

What can you do to make Henry feel welcome?

_____

Kanica has brought some soup to share with the class. She and her family make it at home and it's from Cambodia, where her family is from. You look at the soup and it's like nothing you've ever had before! It smells different from what you're used to. But this is your chance to try something new and interesting. You notice a lot of your classmates scrunch up their noses.

How do you think Kanica feels right now? _____

_____

What can you do? _____

_____

RESPECTING DIFFERENCES

You will be different from your friends. It's a good thing. The differences you have with your friends are interesting things to learn about. But remember, you're more like your friends than you're different.

You might notice differences, though. Being different is your chance to learn. You can learn about other countries, languages, cultures, religions, and ways of living. Maybe you have a friend from India who loves bringing curry to lunch. Curry smells very strong. It might make your nose wrinkle and you ask in a loud voice, "What's that?"

Watch how your friend reacts. Watch your friend's face. Maybe they look down quickly and their voice gets quiet. Instead, they may say with a big smile, "It's curry!"

Some friends will love to celebrate their differences. Other friends may get shy when you point them out. That's why it's so important to watch their faces and walk in their sneakers. How do they feel? How would you feel if someone pointed out something different about you?

It's important to be kind. Welcome the new kid. Say hi! Invite them to play with you. You might learn something new, and they will probably learn something new from you, too.

We're More the Same Than Different

Think of someone you know who might do things differently from you. Maybe they celebrate a holiday you don't. Or they go to church. Or they speak another language.

Write that difference down here:

_____

Now circle all the ways that you're the same. I've left some blank lines so you can add a few of your own.

We're in the same grade.

We live in the same town.

We read the same books.

We watch the same movies and shows.

We like the same games.

We play the same sports.

We each have a brother or a sister.

We have pets.

We're both girls or boys.

_____

_____

_____

Look at how many more ways you're the same than different! Celebrate the differences. Then find something you have in common.

YOU DID IT!

You are learning so much about friendships! What's one new thing you've learned so far in this book? Write it down:

_____

That's amazing, right? Maybe you wrote down one of the things we talked about in this chapter. Let's do a quick review.

You just learned:

- The simple steps of being kind. Waving and smiling go a long way in making other people feel good.

- How to walk in someone else's sneakers. You can tell what someone else might be thinking by watching their face and then thinking how you would feel in the same situation.

- Respecting other people's differences. Celebrate them! Differences are your chance to learn something new. Remember, we are more the same than we are different.

You are ready for the next chapter. Up until now, we've talked about how to talk to friends one-on-one. Now I'm going to teach you the fun and challenges of being in a group of friends.

5.

HAVING FUN IN GROUPS

Do you get a little nervous around groups of people? That's okay. It's normal.

Pretend you see a group of kids playing Frisbee together in the park. Do you ask if you can play, too? Or do you play on your own because you feel scared?

I like to think that fear is really excitement without the breath. When you feel nervous, your body is telling you to take a big belly breath. That's how you can turn that fear into feeling excited to join a group of friends.

And if you don't believe that yet, it's all right. The more you practice, the braver you will feel.

In this chapter, you'll learn about how to join groups of friends, how to ask others to join you, and how to be a good winner and loser. Let's start to play!

JOINING IN

How did you last join a group of friends? Did you say, "Hey, how are you? Can I play?" What did they say? Did they say yes? I hope they did. I would let you join any group that I'm playing in!

And if they didn't say yes, that's okay, too. There are many reasons groups don't let people join. Maybe they're in the middle of a game and just want to finish. Or perhaps they're about to go home soon and you wouldn't have much time to play anyway.

But sometimes they are confused about what you are asking. When people get nervous, they tend to mumble and not make eye contact. Others can't understand them and don't know what they want. I did this a lot when I was younger, because I felt so shy!

Here's what I wish I knew then! If you want to join a group, be bold and friendly and confident.

Confident means that you believe in yourself. You think you are a fun person! Of course a group of people would let you join in!

Here's how to be confident. Stand up straight. Smile big, then go over and:

1. **Ask to join.**
   You can say something simple like, "Can I play with you?" Ask loud and clear so they can understand you.

2. **Show how friendly you are.**

   You do this through your body language.
   (Remember how we talked about that in
   chapter 3?) Smile and make eye contact with each
   group member. If that feels weird, you can always
   look at the spot between their eyes.

3. **Be willing to wait.**

   If a group is in the middle of playing a game,
   they will want to finish it before they let new
   people in. You can say, "That's okay. Can I sit here
   and watch?"

   That's it! Three simple steps to joining a group.

How Often Do You . . . ?

All these friendship skills take time and practice! A little while after I learn something new, I like to check in with myself to see where I am with the skill. That's what you're going to do now.

Rate yourself on how often you do each of the following things. Give yourself a 1 if you never do it, a 2 if you sometimes do it, and a 3 if you always do it.

I ask others to play with me.	1	2	3
I smile at others when I see them.	1	2	3
I wait when friends tell me they can't play right now.	1	2	3
I make eye contact when talking to people.	1	2	3
I ask to join groups.	1	2	3
When I'm in a group, I let other people join us.	1	2	3

How did you do? Circle one of the statements where you gave yourself a 2 or 3. That's something you're strong in! Celebrate that!

Now look at the statements where you gave yourself a 1. Choose one and start practicing it. Make it easy. Maybe you gave yourself a 1 for "I smile at others when I see them." Take a little step and smile at the next person you see.

ASKING OTHERS TO JOIN

Sometimes you may want to make your own group of friends. Maybe you have an idea for a really great game or you want a chance to spend time with certain people. Perhaps you're by yourself at the playground and it would be a lot more fun if you had someone to play with.

You might feel a little nervous asking people to play with you. That's normal! I still feel nervous as a grown-up when I'm somewhere new and I ask someone to join me for lunch or to sit at my table.

It gets better! Now when I ask, I usually know they will say yes because of HOW I ask. Ready to learn?

The most important things to remember are:

1. **Be friendly.**
   It's so simple and I know that I've told you this so many times. That's how important it is! Smile and look at the person in the eyes. Pretend you are already great friends and you're happy to see them again.

2. **Say hi and ask, "Do you want to play with us?"**
   Then wait for them to respond. Usually, they will say, "Sure!" But they might have a few questions.

3. Answer their questions.

If you meet someone at the park, tell them your name! Tell them what you want to play, or ask them what they want to play.

Sometimes you may play with people who don't want to let anyone else play. Pretend you're playing hide-and-seek and your classmate Angelica asks to play. Your friend Jerome says, "No, we're busy right now." You would be happy to let Angelica play, but Jerome said no to her.

If this happens, ask your friend, "Why don't you want to let them play?" Your friend may have a reason. It's your choice to agree or disagree with that reason. If it's something like "I just don't like them," it's good to give people a second chance. Invite them to join your group.

REMEMBER THIS

Keep these few things in mind when joining a group:

- Smile. It helps you look friendly and kind.
- Ask politely. It's important to ask the group's permission to play.
- It's okay if they say, "Not right now." Shrug your shoulders and say "Okay," and then go find someone else to play with.

What Would You Do?

Here are a few situations where kids are joining groups or want to join a group. Read each one and decide what you would do.

Ayanna is playing fortune teller with her friend Daniela. Marcelline walks over to them and asks, "Can I play?" Daniela looks at Ayanna and rolls her eyes. She tells Marcelline, "We're in the middle of something right now." Marcelline slumps her shoulders and walks away.

"Why did you say that?" Ayanna asks Daniela.

"I'm so mad at her!" Daniela explains, "I let her use my crayons in art. She broke them and didn't say she was sorry."

What would you do? _____

_____

Ernie and Cory are playing basketball along with some other kids. Anthony asks to join their game. "Nope!" says Cory. "Last time you played, you told the teacher we didn't share the ball! We had to stop our game." Ernie is quiet and doesn't know what to say.

What would you do?

Ganesa wants to join a group of girls playing on the swings. She feels very nervous! She looks down at the ground and goes over to the girls. She asks quietly, "Can I play?" No one answers her. She doesn't make eye contact and asks a little louder, "Can I play?"

"What?" one of the girls asks.

What would you tell Ganesa she should do to join the group?

BEING A GOOD WINNER AND LOSER

Have you ever played with someone who got mad when they didn't win? I have! Oh, it's not fun.

Pretend you are playing soccer. The whistle blows and you say, "Okay, the game is tied." Your friend gets really mad. They don't want the game to be tied. They want to win. They yell at you.

It doesn't feel good. How do you feel about playing with them again? Not excited? I don't blame you.

What about when you play with someone who brags about winning? "Haha!" they sing. "I won. I won. I won. You lost. I won." That feels yucky, too, right?

It's important when you play with groups to be a good winner and a good loser. Playing games is meant to be fun that you and other people have together. When you win, you may feel really happy. When you lose, it is a bummer. But think about what you want. You want to play games again with people, right? Yes!

Here's what you can do the next time you win *or* lose.

Smile at the end of the game.
Tell everyone you had fun. Ask if they want to play again.

If you won, remember that winning is a little bit of luck and a little bit of skill. Many times, you can't control winning or losing.

Point out what others did well.
This is so good to do when you win! You can say after a game of tag, "You are so fast!" or after a game of basketball, "It was hard to get the ball away from you. Can you teach me how to do that?"

You can always improve by learning from other people. When you win, look at what you can do to get better.

Am I a Good Winner and Loser?

Want to get better at handling winning and losing? Take this quiz to see where you are right now.

1. After I win a game, I:

   a. Talk about how easy it was.

   b. Tell everyone how much fun I had playing.

2. If another player almost beats me, but I win, I:

   a. Say, "Haha, I beat you!"

   b. Tell them they played really well.

3. If I lose a board game, I:

   a. Throw the board game pieces across the room and walk away.

   b. Say, "That was a good game!"

4. How do I treat the winner when I lose? I say:

   a. That's not fair! You cheated!

   b. Congratulations!

Mostly A's: You need practice being a good winner and loser. Remember, it's okay to make mistakes! It takes time to get this right. Practice smiling and congratulating others when you lose. Also, remember to point out the good things others do when you win.

Mostly B's: Your winning and losing skills are awesome! Keep it up!

YOU DID IT!

Whoa! This was a big chapter! Congratulations on making it to the end!

Now you have some skills to practice about how to have fun in groups.

In this chapter, you learned:

- **How to join a group.**
  You now know how to smile and make eye contact. Also, you learned how to ask questions, such as "Can I play with you?"

- **How to ask others to join your group.**
  You now know how to invite others to play. You also learned how to deal with friends who might exclude other people.

- **How to make your own decisions.**
  Remember that you don't have to go along with your friend if they say no to someone playing. Find out the reason they said no and then make your own decision.

- **How to be a good winner and loser.**
  This is so important when playing with groups! The most important thing is to have fun when you play.

We are almost done! In the next chapter, you'll learn about tricky situations like teasing, bullying, and gossiping.

DEALING
WITH TRICKY
SITUATIONS

Have you ever had something happen in a friendship and you didn't know what to do? I have!

Maybe you watched as your friend made fun of a kid in your class. You felt icky but you didn't know how to help. Perhaps you disagreed with your friend about what game to play. Your friend got mad. You got mad, too. Then you didn't talk to each other for a few days.

What do you do in these situations? That's what this chapter is about! We're going to role-play to help you through it! One big thing you'll learn is how to stick up for other people and be kind.

Sometimes it's hard to be kind. Especially when you're angry! But you'll learn to be respectful and handle all these tricky situations like an expert. Ready? Let's begin.

DISAGREEMENTS

You and your friends are not always going to agree with one another. That's okay! Remember that differences make life interesting. And you'll agree with others more often than you don't. But it'll help if you know how to be respectful when you disagree. That means still being kind to a person when you disagree with something they've said. Disagreements are tricky, because some people tend to get mad. That's an easy thing to do! If you feel yourself getting mad, you can use your belly breaths.

Here's what a disagreement may look like.

Pretend you and your friend are eating lunch. You brought a tuna sandwich, which you love. Your friend is eating cucumber slices, which . . . well . . . you think are pretty gross. You wouldn't eat them in a million years. (You may really like cucumber slices in real life, but let's pretend here.)

"Ewwww," your friend says. "Tuna again? That's so yucky."

You're hurt by that. You may feel like crying. But you know it's just a disagreement. So, you take a big belly breath (maybe two) to calm down. You sit up straight. You make eye contact. Then you say in a strong, confident voice, "I know you think that tuna is gross. But I like it. Please respect my opinion." That's it. Then go back to eating your sandwich. You just respectfully disagreed with your friend.

What Would You Do?

Read the following situations and describe what you would do in each.

Jessica and Wendy are playing soccer. Wendy gets the ball and shoots a goal. Jessica screams, "That's not fair; you stole the ball." Wendy looks down and quietly says, "You think I stole the ball, but I played fair." Jessica can't hear her. What would you do if you were Wendy?

Tania and Jovanni always work together in class. One day, Jovanni chooses Nora to work with instead. Tania walks up to Jovanni at recess and says, "I can't believe you didn't work with me! I am so mad at you!" It's okay for Jovanni to work with someone else and still be friends with Tania. What would you do if you were Jovanni?

Francisco and Roger both want the same graphic novel and the library only has one copy! "I got the book first," says Francisco. "Both our hands were on it at the same time!" says Roger. What would you do if you were Francisco?

PEER PRESSURE

Have other people ever tried to make you do something that you don't want to do? Maybe they asked you to climb on top of the monkey bars at the playground. Perhaps they tried to get you to do or say something that could hurt another person's feelings.

This is called peer pressure. A peer is someone who is the same age as you and who you tend to hang out with. Pressure means a push or force. It happens when your friends try to make you do something you don't want to do.

Here are a few tricks that can help you.

1. **First, say something kind.**

   This helps your peer know that you understand what they want. You can say something like:

   "I know you like climbing to the top of the monkey bars," or

   "I know you think it would be funny if we steal their library book."

   That's a good first step, especially if you are having trouble right now saying no to friends.

2. **Then say no.**

   You can follow it by saying why you won't do it, for example:

   "No, I think that would make them feel sad," or

   "No, I don't feel safe doing that," or

"No, my parents have a rule that I need to wear my helmet when I'm riding my bike."
But if you don't feel like explaining, remember that "no" is a complete sentence. You don't have to explain your answer. If you say no and someone asks you why not, you don't have to say anything else.

3. **Walk in someone else's sneakers.**
   I know how it feels to want to do what your friends say. But if they want to do something that makes another person feel bad, use your new skill of empathy.

Look at the person's face. Try to think how you would feel if someone did that to you. That will give you more courage to say no to your friends.

REMEMBER THIS

When friends want you to do something that you don't want to do, remember:

1. Walk in someone else's sneakers. Maybe it's your parents' sneakers if your friends want you to do something dangerous. Maybe it's the sneakers of a kid in class who your friends want you to make fun of.

2. "No" is a complete sentence. You don't need to explain why you don't want to do something.

What Would You Do?

Here are some situations where you might deal with peer pressure. Explain what you would do.

David is new in class. On the first day, he trips over his backpack and everyone laughs. You know it isn't kind. Now your friends dare you to take David's library book and hide it. You know that David was sad when people laughed at him. What can you say to your friends?

First, say something kind:

_____

Then say no and explain why:

_____

Your friend Anya got a new skateboard and she wants you to try it. You've never been on a skateboard before and you're scared. You've seen other people fall off skateboards and it looks like it hurts. Maybe you'll feel ready to try it later, but not right now. Anya really wants to skateboard with you. What can you say?

First, say something kind:

_____

Then say no and explain why:

_____

It's snack time and your friends think it would be fun to go to the bathroom, wet toilet paper, and throw it on the ceiling. "C'mon," they say. "It would be so funny! Wait until you see how it sticks! We won't get caught." You think about the people who will have to clean up the bathroom later. "Hmmmm . . ." you start.

First, say something kind:

_____

Then say no and
explain why:

_____

_____

_____

GOSSIPING

Have you ever played the game telephone? That's when someone starts with a silly saying, like "I like cheese pizza." They whisper it in someone's ear. That person whispers it in the next person's ear. Finally, at the end of the line, the last person says the phrase and it might be "My sister played the piano and licked the wall."

The end is nothing like the beginning! That's what happens when we gossip. Gossiping is spreading stories about other people that may not be true and are often embarrassing.

A good rule is that if you didn't hear it or see it with your own eyes, don't believe it and don't spread it.

Gossip also starts when someone tells a secret that's not meant to be told. Then, when people tell the story over and over again, they get some facts wrong. That can be hurtful, because the story isn't even true!

You can't stop other people from gossiping. But you can stop gossiping yourself.

Pretend someone starts to tell you a story about a classmate tripping on the playground. They laugh as they tell it and say, "Oh, they're always falling down!"

Don't tell the story to anyone else. You might also want to avoid that person who gossips. You can say something simple like, "Oh," and then change the subject: "I'm going to go on the slide."

Maybe a friend comes up to you on the play ground and asks, "Want to hear a secret about the new kid?" You can say, "Nope." Then you can walk in the other direction. It's okay to say that to friends.

What Would You Do?

Read these situations about gossip and describe what you would do.

Lecia and Alana walk out to recess and ask you to come over. They start telling you about your classmate Alex. "Her hair is always so messy!" says Lecia. "Oh my gosh," says Alana, "doesn't she ever brush it?" You know this is gossip, because it's embarrassing to Alex and not kind.

What can you say? _____

_____

Karen leans over her desk in class and taps you on the shoulder. "*Psst*," she says. "I heard a secret about our teacher. Do you want to hear it?" You know that secrets are gossip. You also need to finish your math problems before lunch.

What do you say to Karen? _____

_____

You and Logan heard Dayson tell someone else that his cousin is in jail. "Whoa!" Logan whispers to you. "We need to tell Alek about this!" You know that this is gossip. It's Dayson's secret and you don't think Logan should tell anyone else.

What can you say to Logan? _____

_____

TEASING AND BULLYING

Have you ever teased your friends about something? Maybe you were playing a game and they made a mistake. You said, "Haha! Now the game is mine!"

They might have laughed and said, "Oh! I can't believe I did that!"

In that situation, you were playful teasing. You can tell it's playful because it came from a good place. You respect your friend and you want them to feel happy.

Teasing happens a lot with friends, but watch out for it when it starts to hurt.

If you tease a friend—or if someone teases you—and that teasing makes you feel hurt or embarrassed, that's not okay. If that hurtful teasing happens over and over again, it's called bullying.

A bully wants to embarrass other people. They think that making others feel bad makes them look better and stronger. Let's face it: it's mean.

If someone starts to bully you, make it clear how you feel. You can say, "That's not kind. I'm walking away." Finally, look out for others when they're being bullied. If you notice it, you can tell the bully they're not being kind. You can also tell a grown-up you trust, so they can take care of the situation.

What Would You Do?

Let's role-play with some situations in which you might see teasing and bullying happening. Explain what you would do.

You and your friends are playing jump rope at lunch recess. One of your friends, Ikeem, keeps tripping over the rope. Every time he trips he makes this funny noise and says, "Oh, bananas!" You think this is hilarious! "Haha, Ikeem is bananas!" you say. You look at Ikeem and see that he looks away and is really quiet. Oh no! You realize that he felt hurt from your teasing.

What can you do now? _____

_____

This new section in math is really hard! You're having trouble figuring out how to solve word problems. Your teacher assigns you to work in a group with Kerin. Kerin sees how frustrated you are, then says, "What? I can't believe you don't get this! It's so easy!" You nod and ignore her. The next day, Kerin points at you across the room and says, "Hey! How are the word problems going? I already finished mine! They were so easy!" Kerin is trying to embarrass you to make herself feel better.

What would you do? _____

_____

YOU DID IT!

Wow! I am impressed with all the work you've done.

Tricky situations are hard to deal with. They make many people nervous. But now you are ready. Here are the skills you can use next time a tricky situation pops up.

How to Deal With Disagreements

Remember, the best thing to do is to stay calm. Take a deep belly breath. You can also ask your friend to "please respect my opinion."

What to Do about Gossiping

Gossiping is sharing stories that you've heard about other people. These stories may not even be true. If you hear a story like this, don't share it.

Peer Pressure

It can be hard to say no to peers. Practice saying something kind. Then say no.

Teasing and Bullying

Teasing is playful, but bullying makes people feel weak and embarrassed. When you're teasing someone, pay attention to their face to make sure they're okay. If they look sad, stop teasing them. If you are seeing other people get bullied, go for help.

Oh my goodness! You are almost at the end. Let's finish this book with a big celebration!

7.

YOU'VE GOT THIS!

Yay for you! Clap for yourself! Jump up and down! Have a dance party! Because you made it! You finished the book. I bet it's hard to think of how much you've done and how far you've come. In this book, you learned how to make new friends. You also learned how to be a better friend to those around you.

It may be tricky to remember everything you learned in this book. That's where I got you! Let's finish with a top 10 list of how to have great friendships.

1. **Be yourself.**
   Know what you like to do and share that with your friends.

2. **Stay calm.**
   Some situations with friends will make you mad. That's okay! You can stay calm by taking a belly breath. You can also use flexible thinking to think of solutions that will make you and your friends happy.

3. **Ask questions.**
   The best conversations come from people being interested in each other. Ask your friends questions about themselves. You can ask things like, "What did you do this weekend?" or "What do you think of that book?"

4. **Watch other people's faces.**
   You can tell what people are feeling when you watch their faces. This helps you figure out how to act next.

5. **Pay attention to how your body talks.**
   How are you standing? Are you standing up straight? Are you making eye contact, or looking at that spot between a person's eyes? These all help you look friendly.

6. Think of others.

Kindness goes a long way. Think of what you can do to put a smile on someone's face. Take a walk in their sneakers to figure out what they're feeling.

7. Look for people to include.

Playing in groups can be a lot of fun! Look for people who want someone to play with and invite them to join.

8. Be a good winner and loser.

Congratulate everyone on playing well! Focus on the fun you had instead of winning or losing.

9. You can say no and still be kind.

Peers might want you to do things you don't want to do. You can say something kind, like, "I know you really want me to ride that skateboard. It looks as if it might be fun. I don't want to. I'll watch you do it, though."

10. Be easy on yourself.

Everyone will make mistakes with friends. You might say the wrong thing sometimes. Or you might do something unkind. It's okay! Repair what you did. You might apologize or make up for it some other way. Then forgive yourself.

You're an amazing person! Now go be the best friend you can be.

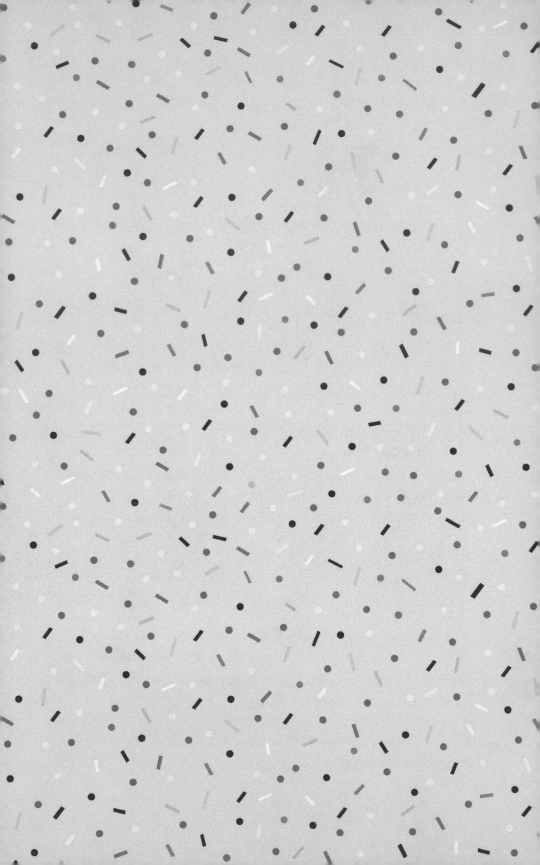

MORE FOR KIDS

Want to practice your new skills? These picture books talk about friendships and being kind to others.

- John, Jory. *The Cool Bean*. HarperCollins, 2019.
- Kuefler, Joseph. *Rulers of the Playground*. Balzer + Bray, 2017.
- Ludwig, Trudy. *The Invisible Boy*. Knopf Books for Young Readers, 2013.
- Palacio, R. J. *We're all Wonders*. Knopf Books for Young Readers, 2017.
- Stein, David Ezra. *Because Amelia Smiled*. Candlewick Press, 2012.

MORE FOR GROWN-UPS

If you would like to help a child develop empathy, self-regulation, and social skills, I highly recommend the following books.

- Borba, Michele. *UnSelfie: Why Empathetic Kids Succeed in Our All-About-Me World*. New York: Touchstone, 2016.

- Monke, Audrey. *Happy Campers: 9 Summer Camp Secrets for Raising Kids Who Become Thriving Adults*. New York: Hachette, 2019.

- Siegel, Daniel J., and Tina Payne Bryson. *The Whole-Brain Child: 12 Revolutionary Strategies to Nurture Your Child's Developing Mind*. New York: Bantam Books, 2012.

- Wiseman, Rosalind. *Queen Bees and Wannabes: Helping Your Daughter Survive Cliques, Gossip, Boyfriends, and the New Realities of Girl World*. New York: Three Rivers Press, 2009.

ACKNOWLEDGMENTS

A huge thank-you to my *No Guilt Mom* podcast partner-in-crime and friend, Brie Tucker, for having huge in-depth conversations on what's best for kids and how to best support parents.

My heartfelt appreciation to Dr. Michele Borba, Dr. Tina Payne Bryson, Katie Hurley, Jessica Lahey, Ned Johnson, KJ Dell'Antonia, Phyllis Fagell, Debbie Reber, Sheryl Ziegler, Tessa Stuckey, Katherine Reynolds Lewis, and Audrey Monke, for taking the time to chat and share your wisdom.

And finally, a big thank-you to my family. Josh, my husband and best friend, your love and support keep me going. My parents, Jim and Mary, for raising me to care for others. My sister, Jamie; sister-in-law, Melissa; mom-in-law, Leslie; dad-in-law, Dave; and brothers-in-law, Nick and Kory, for helping me celebrate my wins. And to my kids, Camdyn and Erik, you let me into your world and show me how I can best help other kids. I love you all!

ABOUT THE AUTHOR

 **JoAnn Crohn** is a former elementary school teacher with a master's degree in curriculum and instruction as well as a National Board Certified Teacher in middle childhood education. After teaching in public schools, she now runs the parenting company No Guilt Mom (NoGuiltMom.com), where she helps parents raise self-sufficient kids. She's also the host of the *No Guilt Mom* podcast and author of the book *Drama Free Homework: A Parent's Guide to Eliminating Homework Battles and Raising Focused Kids*. She lives in Chandler, Arizona.

Printed in the USA
CPSIA information can be obtained
at www.ICGtesting.com
CBHW082046220524
8972CB00009B/166

9 781648 768088